BOOK TWO

HAL LEONARD
GUITAR TAB METHOD

Written by Jeff Schroedl

Contributing Editors: Jeff Arnold, Kurt Plahna, and Jim Schustedt

PLAYBACK+
Speed • Pitch • Balance • Loop

To access audio, visit:
www.halleonard.com/mylibrary

Enter Code
4767-2057-7925-0611

ISBN 978-1-4584-2192-0

Visit Hal Leonard Online at
www.halleonard.com

World headquarters, contact:
Hal Leonard
7777 West Bluemound Road
Milwaukee, WI 53213
Email: info@halleonard.com

In Europe, contact:
Hal Leonard Europe Limited
1 Red Place
London, W1K 6PL
Email: info@halleonardeurope.com

In Australia, contact:
Hal Leonard Australia Pty. Ltd.
4 Lentara Court
Cheltenham, Victoria, 3192 Australia
Email: info@halleonard.com.au

MOVIN' UP THE FRETBOARD

In Book One, we learned all of the notes within the first five frets. Now let's move beyond first position and start playing "up the neck." Here are the notes within frets 5–12 on the low three strings.

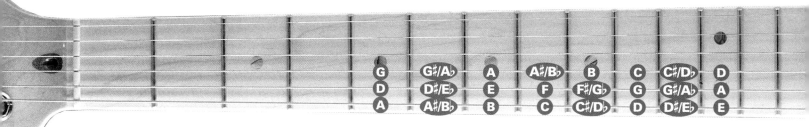

SUNSHINE OF YOUR LOVE

Eric Clapton played the immortal riff in this song with the band Cream. Use your 3rd finger to fret the first note. Then, for the final three notes, shift down two frets to use your 3rd finger (low D) and 1st finger (F).

RUNNIN' DOWN A DREAM

Use **alternate picking** to play this Tom Petty riff up to speed. This simply means to alternate between downstrokes (⊓) and upstrokes (∨). For this riff, start with an upstroke.

MISIRLOU

This Dick Dale surf-rock classic is fun to play on the low E string. Experiment with different fingerings, and use alternate picking to help you play more quickly. After you pick the last note, quickly slide your fret-hand finger down the string (to no particular fret).

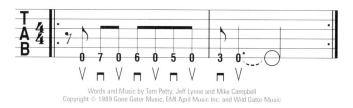

DON'T STOP BELIEVIN'

Here's a riff by the band Journey that jumps between two areas of the fretboard. Notice that the same note can be played at different locations. The last note of the 1st measure is the same low B as the first note of the 2nd measure.

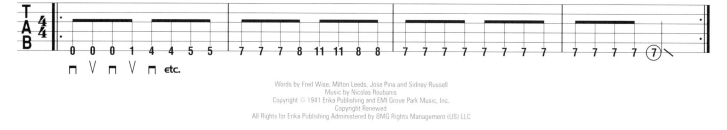

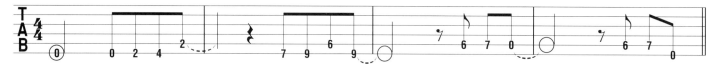

I HATE MYSELF FOR LOVING YOU

Power chords can be played "up the neck," too. The same two-finger shape is named by where the 1st finger is positioned. Here's a popular riff from the 1980s that features power chords with roots along the 5th string. Fret the 6th-string notes with your middle finger.

JESSIE'S GIRL

Rick Springfield's #1 hit provides more power chord practice.

P.M. throughout

ROCK YOU LIKE A HURRICANE

The German hard rock group Scorpions used power chords for this popular rock anthem.

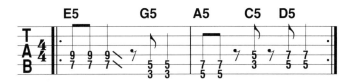

TALK DIRTY TO ME

This famous intro by the band Poison makes use of a common rhythm guitar technique known as **muffled strings**, or "scratches." When you see X's in tab, lift your fret-hand fingers just enough to prevent the notes from sounding. A percussive, "dead" sound will then result as you pick the strings.

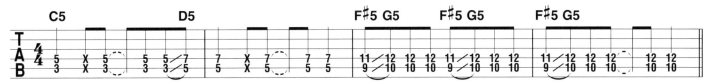

You've already learned that a dot after a note increases the value by one half. Therefore a **dotted quarter note** lasts for 1-1/2 beats.

WHEREVER I MAY ROAM

Now let's mix notes and power chords all along the fretboard with hammer-ons, slides, and dotted quarter notes.

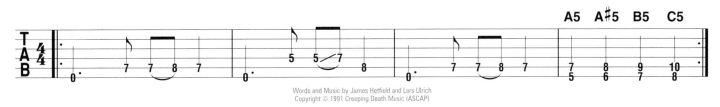

MOVIN' UP THE FRETBOARD: PART 2

Here are the notes within frets 5–12 on the high three strings.

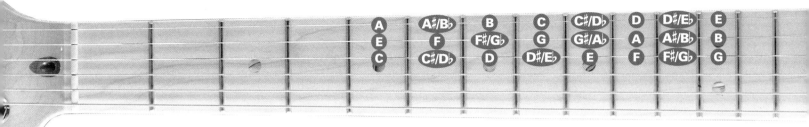

PURPLE HAZE

Jimi Hendrix's legendary riff is a must-know for all guitarists. For the first four notes, use fingers 3, 1, 2, and 1, respectively.

GET READY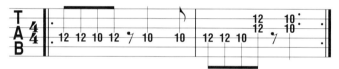

This driving Motown hit makes good use of **double stops** (or dyads), which is a term borrowed from violin technique that means to pick two notes together. Flatten your finger to depress both notes simultaneously.

UP AROUND THE BEND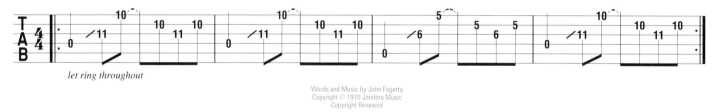

Here's a famous guitar intro by Creedence Clearwater Revival. Use your 2nd finger to play the slides and notes on the 3rd string, and lay your 1st finger across the top two strings to fret the notes at the 10th and 5th frets. Slide into the notes quickly from no particular starting point.

let ring throughout

MAMA, I'M COMING HOME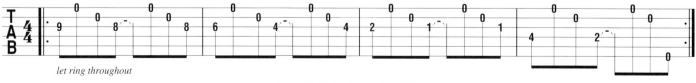

Guitarist Zakk Wylde played the descending guitar riff on this Ozzy Osbourne song. Arch your fingers and play on the tips to allow the open strings to ring out.

let ring throughout

THE MUNSTERS THEME 🔊

The sinister-sounding melody from this TV sitcom is fun to play, and provides more practice for playing "up" the neck.

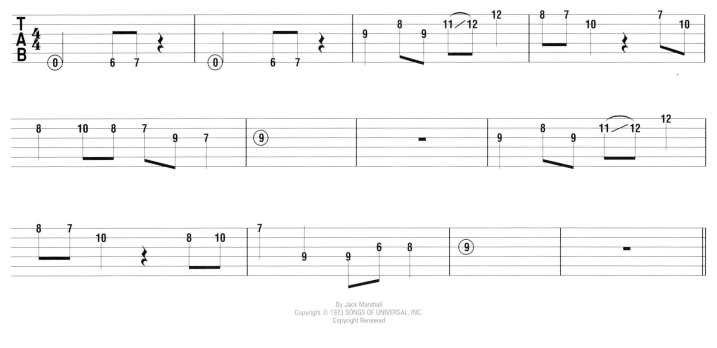

By Jack Marshall
Copyright © 1973 SONGS OF UNIVERSAL, INC.
Copyright Renewed

HAWAII FIVE-O THEME 🔊

Here's another popular TV tune. It was an instrumental hit for the Ventures in 1969, and is still often heard at sporting events. This one moves quickly, so be sure to use alternate picking.

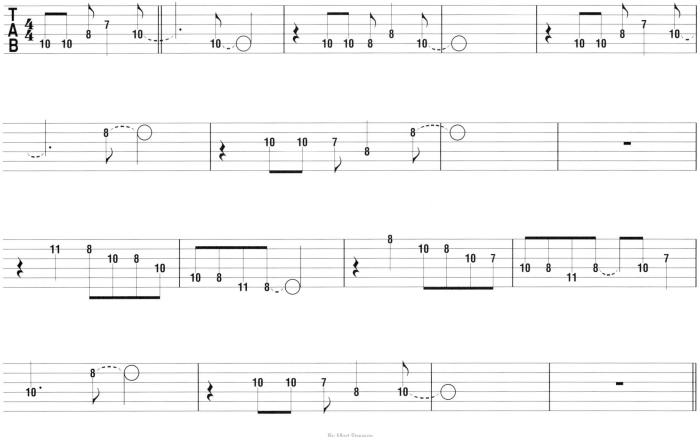

By Mort Stevens
Copyright © 1969 Sony/ATV Music Publishing LLC and Aspenfair Music
Copyright Renewed
All Rights Administered by Sony/ATV Music Publishing LLC, 8 Music Square West, Nashville, TN 37203

HE'S A PIRATE

The theme from the movie series *Pirates of the Caribbean* is played in 3/4 time. Once again, use alternate picking for the eighth notes. Also, be sure to apply vibrato when it's notated.

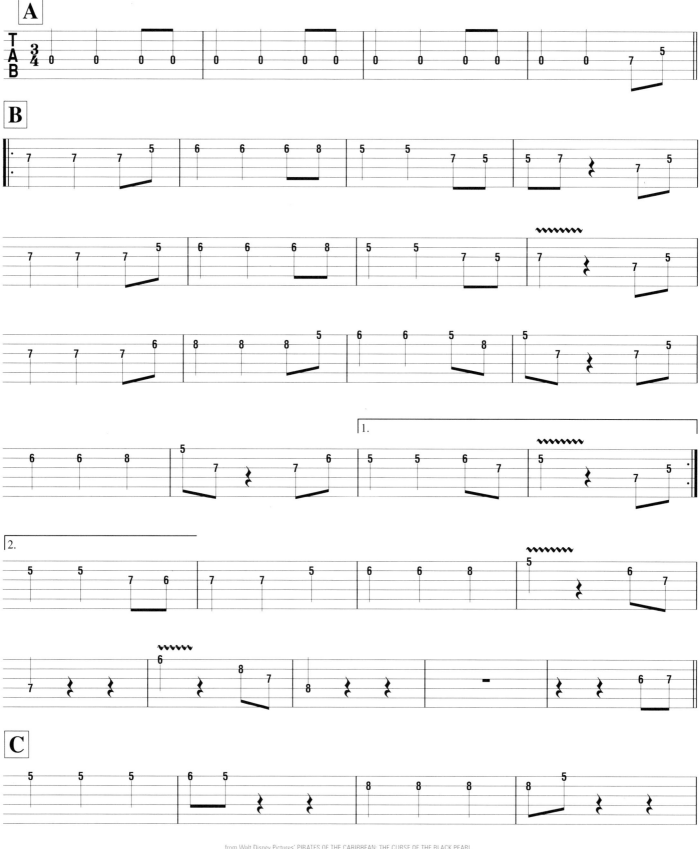

from Walt Disney Pictures' PIRATES OF THE CARIBBEAN: THE CURSE OF THE BLACK PEARL
Music by Klaus Badelt
© 2003 Walt Disney Music Company

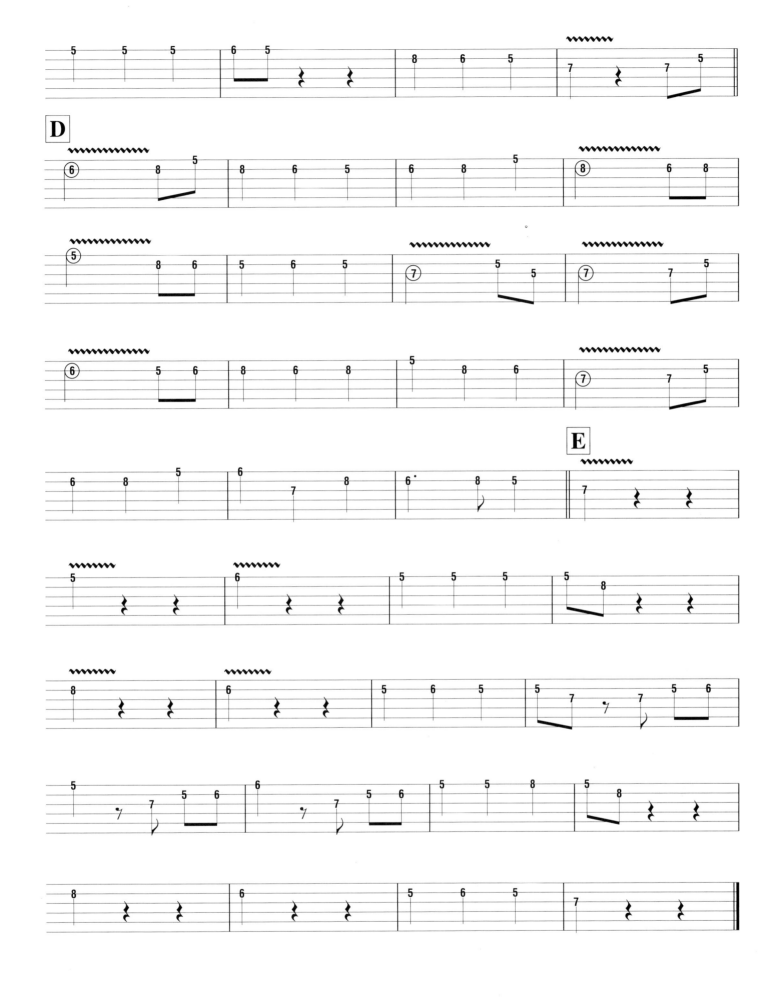

NEW RHYTHMS

A **sixteenth note** lasts half as long as an eighth note, and is written with two flags or two beams. There are four sixteenth notes in one beat.

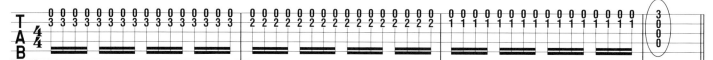

= 1/4 beat   = 1/2 beat   = 1 beat

HELTER SKELTER

The raucous intro to this song by the Beatles uses sixteenth notes. Divide the beat into four, and count "one-e-and-a, two-e-and-a, three-e-and-a, four-e-and-a."

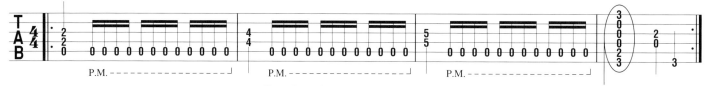

Count: 1-e-and-a 2-e-and-a etc.

I DON'T KNOW

Ready for some faster picking? Play the sixteenth notes on the open A string using steady, alternating downstrokes and upstrokes. Also apply palm muting to sound more like the original Ozzy Osbourne recording.

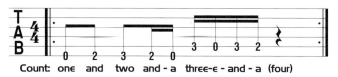

P.M. ------------   P.M. ------------   P.M. ------------

ROCK LOBSTER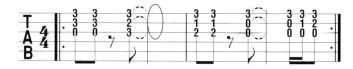

Here's a fun riff by the B-52's. The second beat mixes an eighth note and two sixteenths.

Count: one and two and - a three-e - and - a (four)

PLUSH

This song by Stone Temple Pilots features one of the most recognizable riffs of the 1990s.

THE TROOPER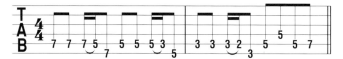

Use pull-offs to help you play Iron Maiden's signature riff up to full speed.

THE JOKER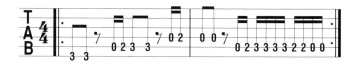

This song by the Steve Miller Band was a #1 hit in 1974.

THEME FROM KING OF THE HILL

The galloping guitar riff in the theme from this animated TV series sounds cool and also serves as a great picking exercise.

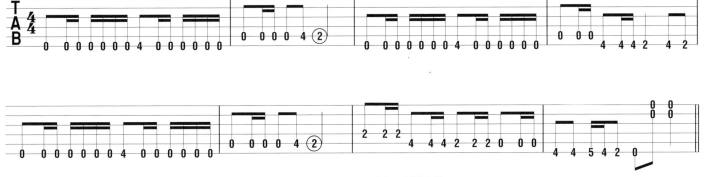

from the Twentieth Century Fox Television Series KING OF THE HILL
By Roger Clyne, Brian Blush, Arthur Edwards and Paul Naffah
Copyright © 1997 T C F Music Publishing, Inc.

IRON MAN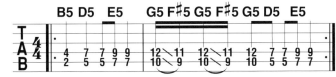

Now let's try sixteenths with power chords in Black Sabbath's all-time classic metal track.

Words and Music by Frank Iommi, John Osbourne, William Ward and Terence Butler
© Copyright 1970 (Renewed) and 1974 (Renewed) Westminster Music Ltd., London, England
TRO - Essex Music International, Inc., New York, controls all publication rights for the U.S.A. and Canada

MY BEST FRIEND'S GIRL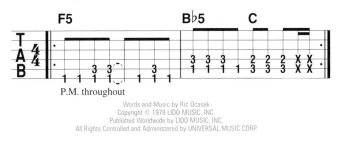

This riff by the Cars uses muffled sixteenths in transition from the C dyad back to F.

Words and Music by Ric Ocasek
Copyright © 1978 LIDO MUSIC, INC.
Published Worldwide by LIDO MUSIC, INC.
All Rights Controlled and Administered by UNIVERSAL MUSIC CORP.

SOUTH OF HEAVEN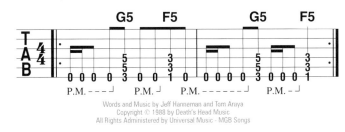

For a fuller sound, power chords can be expanded to three notes. Try playing the reinforced shape on this riff by the band Slayer.

Words and Music by Jeff Hanneman and Tom Araya
Copyright © 1988 by Death's Head Music
All Rights Administered by Universal Music - MGB Songs

AMERICAN WOMAN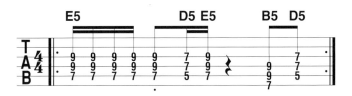

The Guess Who's #1 hit also puts three-note power chords to good use.

Written by Burton Cummings, Randy Bachman, Gary Peterson and Jim Kale
© 1970 (Renewed 1998) SHILLELAGH MUSIC (BMI)
All Rights Administered by BUG MUSIC, INC., a BMG CHRYSALIS COMPANY

BARRACUDA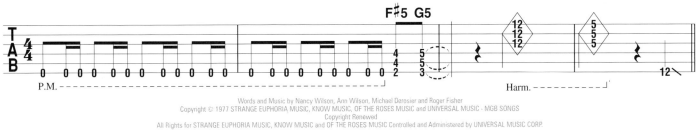

The hard rock song "Barracuda" is the band Heart's signature song. Its aggressive opening riff uses sixteenth notes and **natural harmonics**. When you see "Harm." under the tab and diamonds around the tab numbers, pick the strings while the fret-hand lightly touches the strings directly over the metal fret wire. Natural harmonics produce bell-like, chiming tones.

Words and Music by Nancy Wilson, Ann Wilson, Michael Derosier and Roger Fisher
Copyright © 1977 STRANGE EUPHORIA MUSIC, KNOW MUSIC, OF THE ROSES MUSIC and UNIVERSAL MUSIC - MGB SONGS
Copyright Renewed
All Rights for STRANGE EUPHORIA MUSIC, KNOW MUSIC and OF THE ROSES MUSIC Controlled and Administered by UNIVERSAL MUSIC CORP.

CHANGES

Jimi Hendrix recorded this song on the famous live album, *Band of Gypsys*. Two of the guitar riffs are repeated several times. To avoid tabbing the same parts over and over again, riffs and/or rhythm figures are often labeled and recalled.

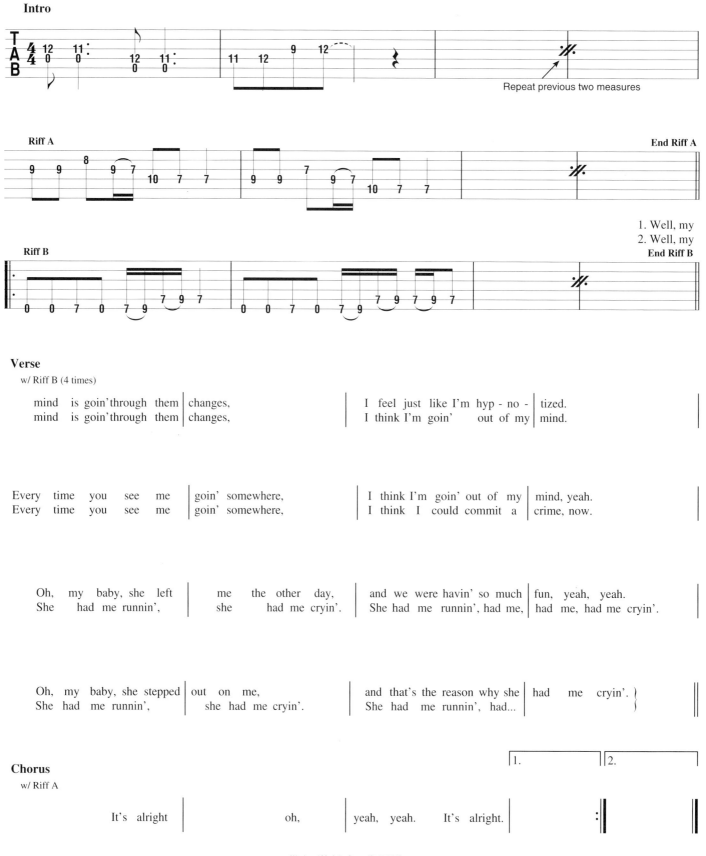

Words and Music by George "Buddy" Miles
© 1967 (Renewed) MILES AHEAD MUSIC (ASCAP)

A **triplet** is a group of three notes played in the space of two. Whereas eighth notes divide a beat into two parts, **eighth-note triplets** divide a beat into three parts.

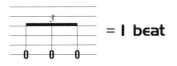 = 1 beat

ADDAMS FAMILY THEME

While playing the riff from this classic TV show, count your new rhythm by simply saying the word "tri-pl-et."

Count: tri - pl - et   one   (two three)   tri - pl - et   one   etc.

AM I EVIL?

Triplets fuel the menacing sound of this riff. Metallica's famous cover version is considered one of the heaviest metal tracks ever.

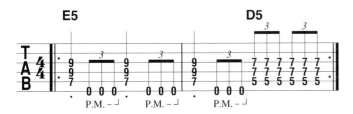

SPANISH BOLERO

Musicians from Maurice Ravel to Jeff Beck have made use of this rhythm. The chord movement is easy; just slide the open E chord shape.

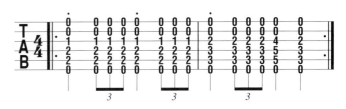

JESU, JOY OF MAN'S DESIRING

Here's a well-known classical piece that uses triplets in 3/4 time.

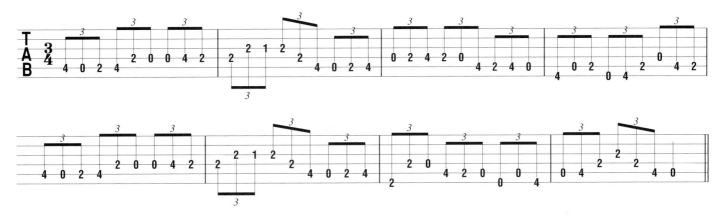

A **shuffle** is a bouncy, skipping rhythm. Eighth notes are played as long-short, rather than as equal values. The feel is the same as inserting a rest in the middle of a triplet.

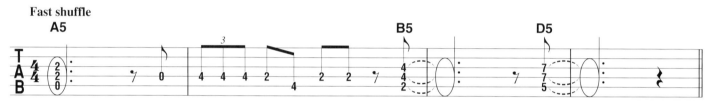

YOU SHOOK ME

Muddy Waters, Led Zeppelin, and others recorded this popular blues song.

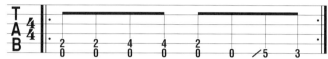

PRIDE AND JOY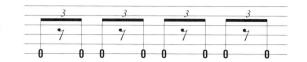

Here's the main riff of blues guitar hero Stevie Ray Vaughan's signature song. Use alternate picking.

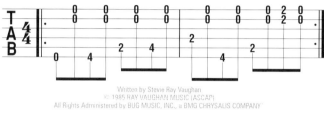

THE BOYS ARE BACK IN TOWN

Now let's mix shuffled eighth notes and triplets to play a rock classic by Thin Lizzy.

THAT'LL BE THE DAY

This Buddy Holly hit is one of early rock 'n' roll's most enduring songs.

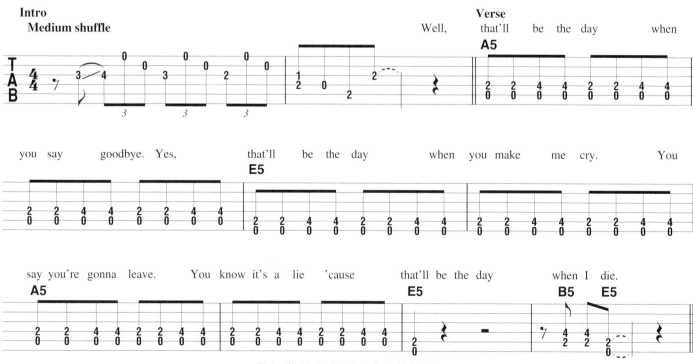

THE PINK PANTHER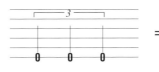

Henry Mancini was one of the greatest composers of the 20th century. "The Pink Panther" is a shuffle that uses triplets, pull-offs, slides, and notes on all six strings.

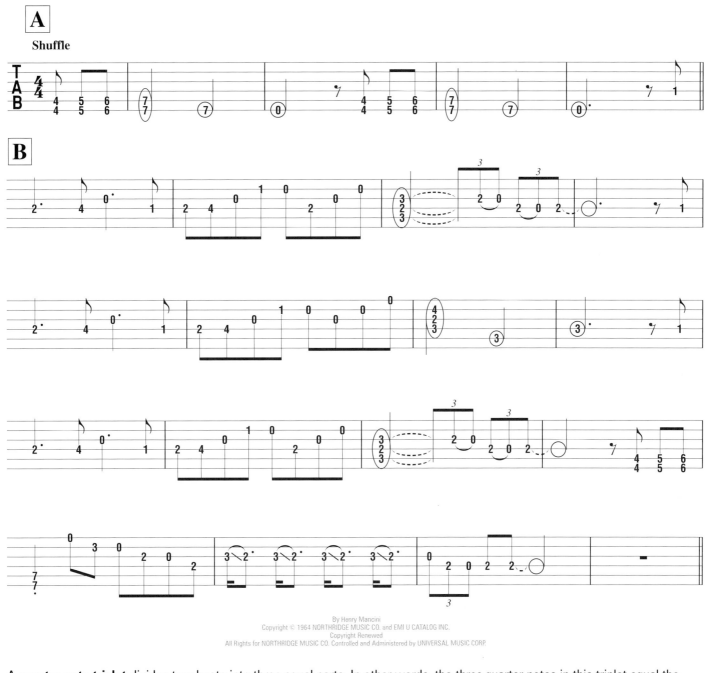

A **quarter-note triplet** divides two beats into three equal parts. In other words, the three quarter notes in this triplet equal the same time as two regular quarter notes.

= 2 beats

SEVEN NATION ARMY

Observe the counting below the tab of this riff by the White Stripes.

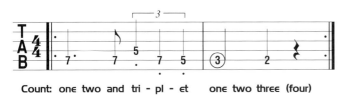

Count: one two and tri - pl - et   one two three (four)

HOLD THE LINE

The band Toto scored their first hit with "Hold the Line."

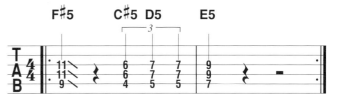

DETROIT ROCK CITY 🔊

Now try your hand at playing another full song. Here's a vintage favorite by the band Kiss.

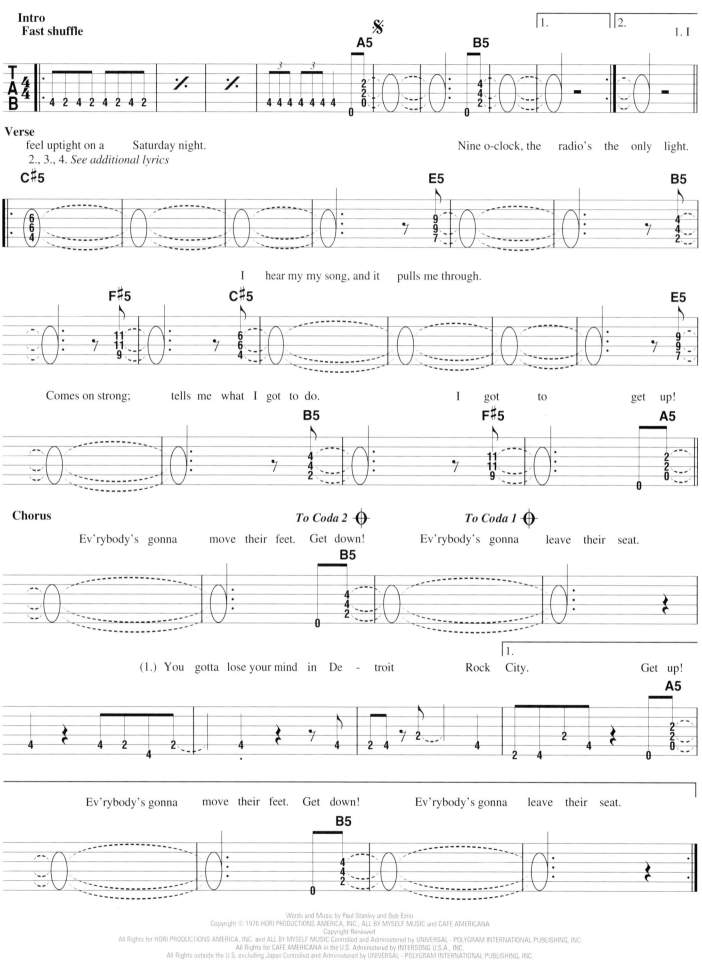

Intro
Fast shuffle

Verse

feel uptight on a   Saturday night.
2., 3., 4. *See additional lyrics*

Nine o-clock, the   radio's   the   only   light.

I   hear my my song, and it   pulls me through.

Comes on strong;   tells me what I got to do.   I   got   to   get   up!

Chorus

To Coda 2 ⊕   *To Coda 1* ⊕

Ev'rybody's gonna   move their feet. Get down!   Ev'rybody's gonna   leave their seat.

(1.) You   gotta   lose your mind in De - troit   Rock   City.   Get up!

Ev'rybody's gonna   move their feet. Get down!   Ev'rybody's gonna   leave their seat.

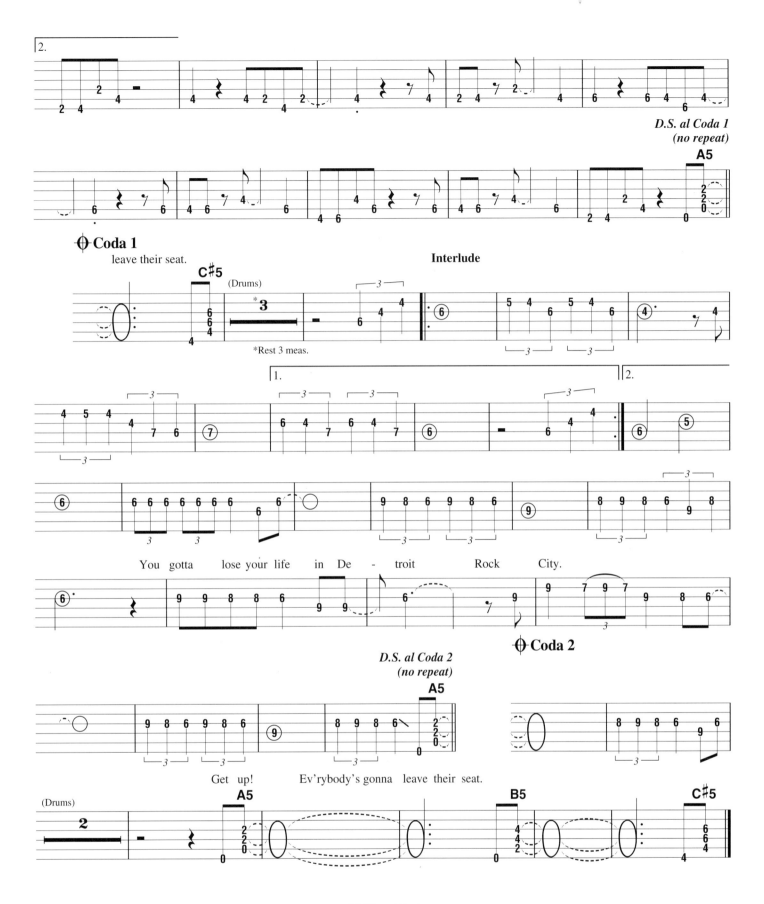

Additional Lyrics

2. Gettin' late, I just can't wait.
   Ten o'clock, and I know I gotta hit the road.
   First I drink, then I smoke.
   Start up the car,
   And I try to make the midnight show. Get up!

3. Movin' fast down Ninety-Five.
   I hit top speed,
   But I'm still movin' much too slow.
   I feel so good; I'm so alive.
   Hear my song playin' on the radio.
   It goes: get up!

4. Twelve o'clock, I gotta rock.
   There's a truck ahead,
   Lights starin' at my eyes.
   Whoa, my God, no time to turn.
   I got to laugh, 'cause I know I'm gonna die.
   Why? Get up!

THE MAJOR SCALE

A **scale** is a succession of notes ascending or descending in a specific order. The most common scale is the **major scale**. It can be built starting on any root note, and follows a specific pattern of **whole steps** (two frets) and **half steps** (one fret). Here it is beginning on the low E.

E MAJOR SCALE

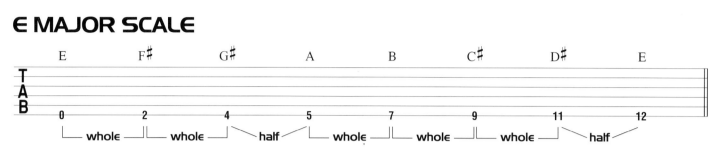

Although it's easy to visualize the scale pattern across one string, it's not practical to play it this way. Here is the standard fingering for playing the major scale on the guitar.

G MAJOR SCALE

The scale above starts on the note G, so it's a G major scale. If you move the pattern up two frets, it becomes an A major scale.

A MAJOR SCALE

You can apply this movable major scale pattern to any root note along the low string. The pattern should be practiced, with alternate picking, ascending and descending.

Here's another way to visualize the movable pattern:

Major Scale Pattern 1 – Root on 6th String

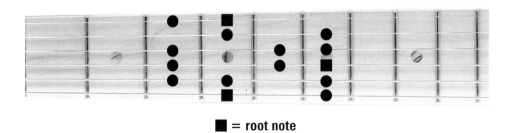

■ = root note

Practicing scales is a good way to develop fret-hand technique. Start slowly, and gradually build up speed.

The notes of the major scale are the foundation for countless melodies, riffs, solos, and chord progressions. Here are a few examples.

DO-RE-MI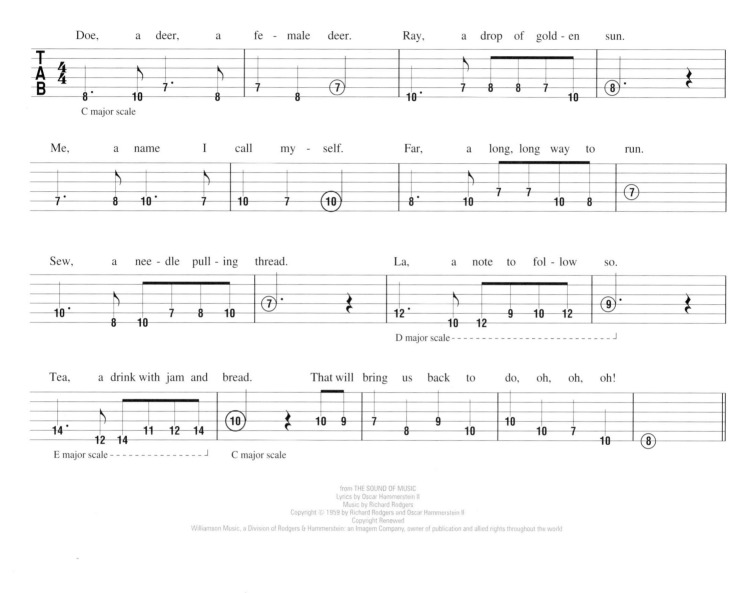

This Rodgers and Hammerstein song from *The Sound of Music* is arguably the most famous use of the major scale in popular music. The lyrics also teach the seven solfège syllables commonly used to sing the major scale. The melody uses mostly notes from the C major scale, and shifts briefly to D major and E major in measures 11 and 13, respectively.

from THE SOUND OF MUSIC
Lyrics by Oscar Hammerstein II
Music by Richard Rodgers
Copyright © 1959 by Richard Rodgers and Oscar Hammerstein II
Copyright Renewed
Williamson Music, a Division of Rodgers & Hammerstein: an Imagem Company, owner of publication and allied rights throughout the world

HELLO, GOODBYE

The main riff in the chorus of this song by the Beatles runs straight up the C major scale, tabbed here in open position.

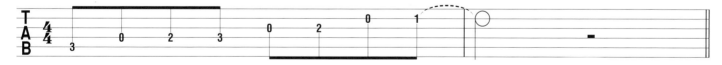

Words and Music by John Lennon and Paul McCartney
Copyright © 1967 Sony/ATV Music Publishing LLC
Copyright Renewed
All Rights Administered by Sony/ATV Music Publishing LLC, 8 Music Square West, Nashville, TN 37203

There are many patterns for playing the major scale on the guitar. Here's one with three notes per string that has its root on the 5th string. Let's try it in D.

D MAJOR SCALE

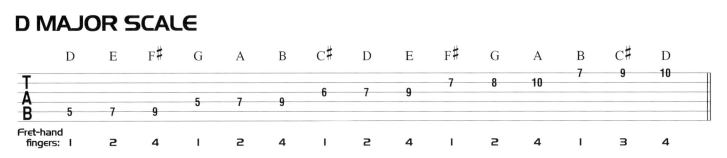

To help you visualize the pattern, here it is on the fretboard:

Major Scale Pattern 2 – Root on 5th String

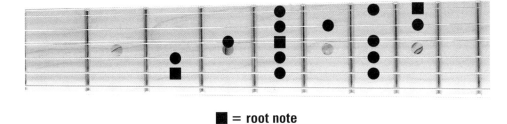

■ = root note

JOY TO THE WORLD 🔊

The melody of this famous Christmas carol, by Baroque composer George Frideric Handel, uses all of the notes in the D major scale.

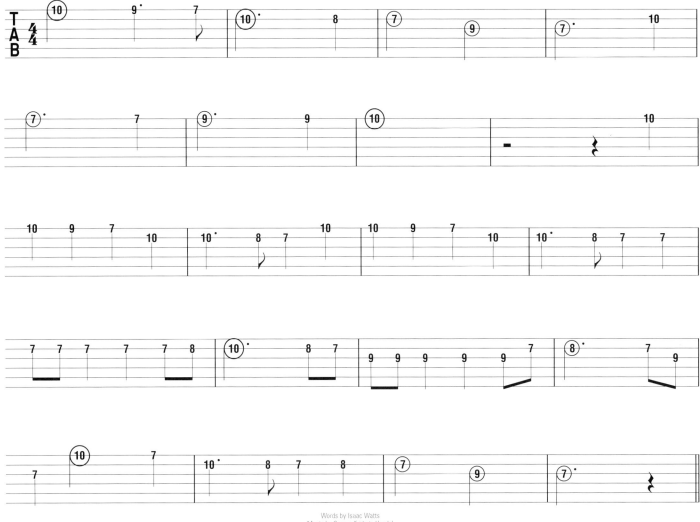

MUSIC THEORY 101

When we see that the notes of a particular song come from a certain scale, we say that the song is in the **key** of that scale. For instance, if the notes of a song all come from the C major scale, we say that the song is in the key of C major.

GOODBYE TO ROMANCE

The intro to "Goodbye to Romance" by Ozzy Osbourne uses notes exclusively from the D major scale:

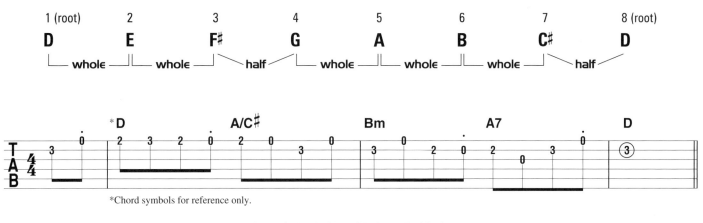

*Chord symbols for reference only.

Words and Music by John Osbourne, Robert Daisley and Randy Rhoads
TRO - © Copyright 1981 and 1984 Essex Music International, Inc., New York and Blizzard Music, Daytona Beach, FL

Notice how the guitar part seems to be "at rest" when you arrive at the last note (D)? This is because the D note is the root, or **tonic**—the note around which the key revolves.

MAJOR SCALE CHART

Major scales are the building blocks of music, and music theory. Chords and chord progressions are also derived from scales. Following is a handy table that spells the notes in all 12 keys. Don't get bogged down trying to memorize all this at once, but you might want to dog-ear this page for future reference.

	1 (root)	2	3	4	5	6	7
C major	C	D	E	F	G	A	B
G major	G	A	B	C	D	E	F♯
D major	D	E	F♯	G	A	B	C♯
A major	A	B	C♯	D	E	F♯	G♯
E major	E	F♯	G♯	A	B	C♯	D♯
B major	B	C♯	D♯	E	F♯	G♯	A♯
F♯ major	F♯	G♯	A♯	B	C♯	D♯	E♯
D♭ major	D♭	E♭	F	G♭	A♭	B♭	C
A♭ major	A♭	B♭	C	D♭	E♭	F	G
E♭ major	E♭	F	G	A♭	B♭	C	D
B♭ major	B♭	C	D	E♭	F	G	A
F major	F	G	A	B♭	C	D	E

THE F CHORD

The F chord uses no open strings, and it also requires the use of a **barre** (pronounced "bar"). Barring is done by flattening a finger across more than one string at a time. Here, use your 1st finger to press down the 1st and 2nd strings. Adjust the angle of your finger, or rotate your finger slightly on its side as necessary, so the notes sound clearly. Fret the remaining two notes with your 2nd and 3rd fingers as shown.

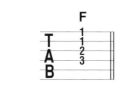

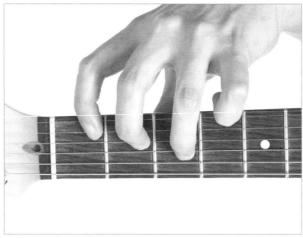

FREE BIRD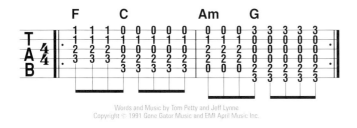

Let's take it slow with your new chord, and try playing it in the chord progression of Lynyrd Skynyrd's classic rock ballad.

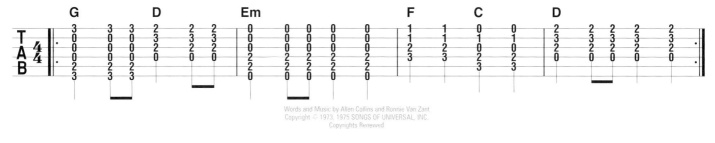

Words and Music by Allen Collins and Ronnie Van Zant
Copyright © 1973, 1975 SONGS OF UNIVERSAL, INC.
Copyrights Renewed

LEARNING TO FLY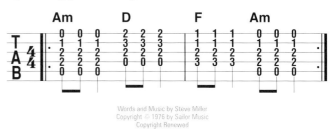

Tom Petty's acoustic hit uses four chords, including F, in steady eighth-note strums.

FLY LIKE AN EAGLE

Steve Miller's 1977 hit can be played with just three chords: Am, D, and F. First try the tabbed strum pattern, and then try improvising your own right-hand strums.

Words and Music by Tom Petty and Jeff Lynne
Copyright © 1991 Gone Gator Music and EMI April Music Inc.

Words and Music by Steve Miller
Copyright © 1976 by Sailor Music
Copyright Renewed

LIKE A ROLLING STONE

Bob Dylan's iconic song is fun to strum. Again, feel free to vary your right-hand strumming as it feels natural to you.

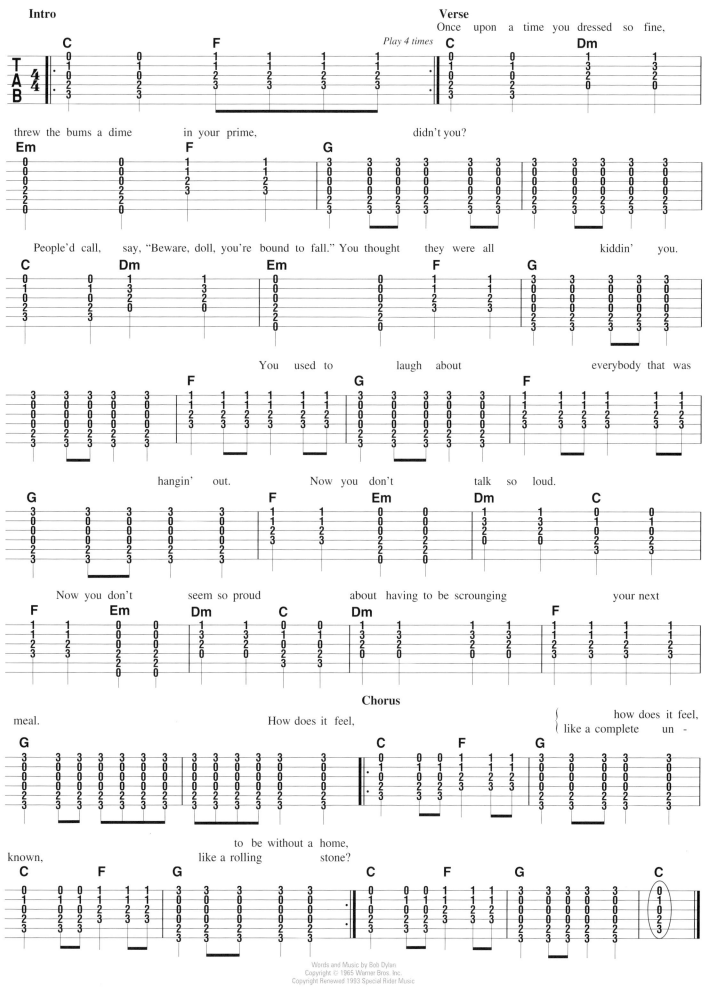

SEVENTH CHORDS

Seventh chords are comprised of four different notes. They sound richer than ordinary major and minor chords that contain three notes, but are generally not more difficult to play. The most common type of seventh chord is the **dominant seventh**. It is built from the root, 3rd, 5th, and flat-7th **degrees** (notes) of the major scale, and its chord label simply includes the suffix "7."

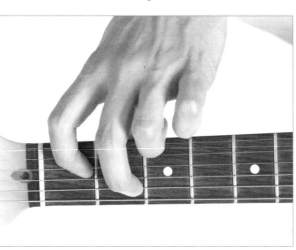

LOVE ME TENDER

Strum once per beat to play this #1 hit ballad by Elvis Presley.

Love me tender, love me sweet. Never let me go.
You have made my life complete and I love you so.

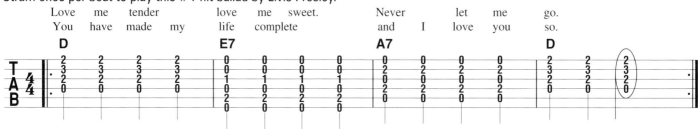

Words and Music by Elvis Presley and Vera Matson
Copyright © 1956; Renewed 1984 Elvis Presley Music (BMI)
Worldwide Rights for Elvis Presley Music Administered by BMG Rights Management (US) LLC

TAKE ME TO THE RIVER

Al Green's 1974 hit has been recorded by many artists. Use your 1st finger to press (or barre) all the notes of the A chord in the song's main groove.

Words and Music by Al Green and Mabon Hodges
Copyright © 1974 IRVING MUSIC, INC. and AL GREEN MUSIC, INC.
Copyright Renewed
All Rights Controlled and Administered by IRVING MUSIC, INC.

SMOOTH

Carlos Santana and Rob Thomas collaborated on this Latin-style, Grammy-winning hit. Here's the main chord progression.

Words by Rob Thomas
Music by Rob Thomas and Itaal Shur
© 1999 EMI BLACKWOOD MUSIC INC., BIDNIS, INC. and ITAAL SHUR MUSIC
All Rights for BIDNIS, INC. Controlled and Administered by EMI BLACKWOOD MUSIC INC.

TWIST AND SHOUT

Now try a song recorded by the Beatles that changes chords more quickly.

Shake it up baby, now.   Twist and shout.   Come on, come on, come on
baby, now.   Come on and work it on out.

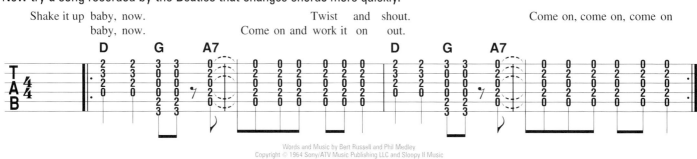

Words and Music by Bert Russell and Phil Medley
Copyright © 1964 Sony/ATV Music Publishing LLC and Sloopy II Music
Copyright Renewed
All Rights on behalf of Sony/ATV Music Publishing LLC Administered by Sony/ATV Music Publishing LLC, 8 Music Square West, Nashville, TN 37203

D7

 G7

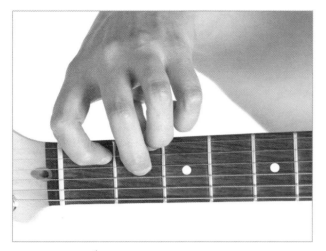

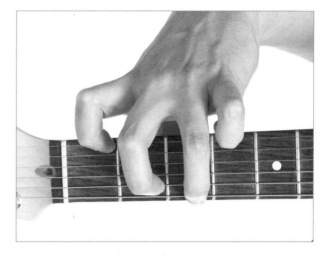

TAXMAN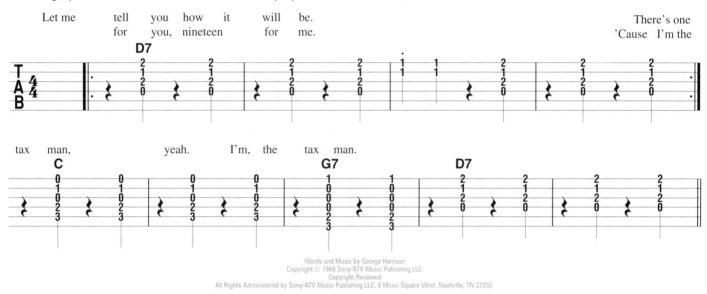

This song by the Beatles features seventh chords played on the "backbeat," or beats 2 and 4 of most measures.

Let me tell you how it will be.   There's one
for you, nineteen for me.   'Cause I'm the

tax man,   yeah.   I'm, the tax man.

FIVE FOOT TWO, EYES OF BLUE

The California Ramblers recorded the original version of this fun big band hit in 1925. Remember that a "shuffle" means to strum the eighth notes with a long-short feel.

Shuffle

1. Five foot two,   eyes of blue,   but oh what those five   foot could do.   Has
2. Turned up nose,   turned down hose,   never had no   other beaus.   }

an-y-bod-y seen my girl?

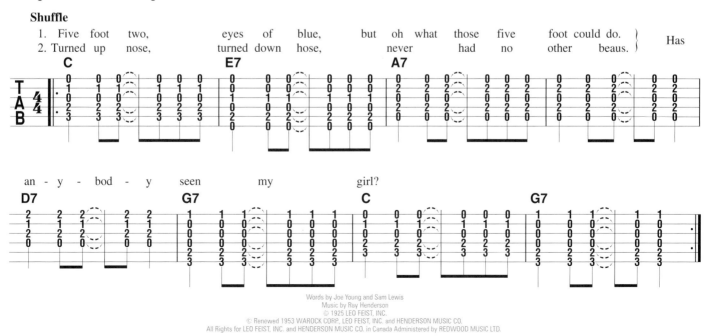

C7

B7

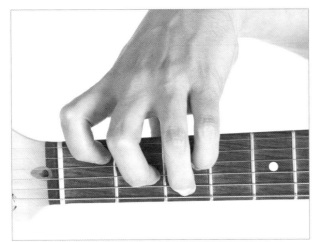

ALL I WANNA DO

Sheryl Crow's breakthrough hit won a Grammy for "Record of the Year" in 1995.

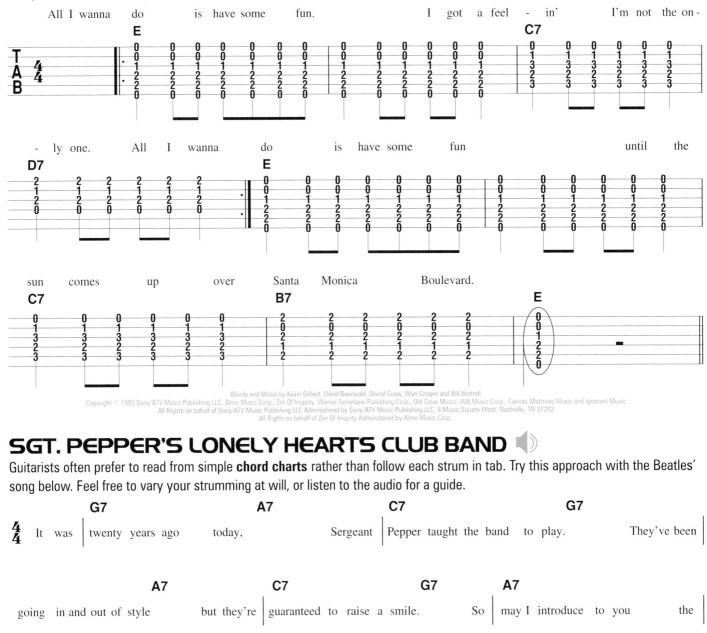

Words and Music by Kevin Gilbert, David Baerwald, Sheryl Crow, Wyn Cooper and Bill Bottrell
Copyright © 1993 Sony/ATV Music Publishing LLC, Almo Music Corp., Zen Of Iniquity, Warner-Tamerlane Publishing Corp., Old Crow Music, WB Music Corp., Canvas Mattress Music and Ignorant Music
All Rights on behalf of Sony/ATV Music Publishing LLC Administered by Sony/ATV Music Publishing LLC, 8 Music Square West, Nashville, TN 37203
All Rights on behalf of Zen Of Iniquity Administered by Almo Music Corp.

SGT. PEPPER'S LONELY HEARTS CLUB BAND

Guitarists often prefer to read from simple **chord charts** rather than follow each strum in tab. Try this approach with the Beatles' song below. Feel free to vary your strumming at will, or listen to the audio for a guide.

	G7		A7	C7		G7	
$\frac{4}{4}$ It was	twenty years ago	today,	Sergeant	Pepper taught the band	to play.		They've been

	A7		C7		G7	A7	
going in and out of style	but they're	guaranteed to raise a smile.	So	may I introduce	to you		the

	C7		G7	C7		G7	
act you've known for all these years?		Sergeant	Pepper's	Lonely Hearts Club Band.			

Words and Music by John Lennon and Paul McCartney
Copyright © 1967 Sony/ATV Music Publishing LLC
Copyright Renewed
All Rights Administered by Sony/ATV Music Publishing LLC, 8 Music Square West, Nashville, TN 37203

I SAW HER STANDING THERE 🔊

Here's another song by the Beatles that makes good use of seventh chords. Once again, follow the chord symbols and ad lib. your strumming.

Verse

$\frac{4}{4}$

|| E7 | | A7 | E7 |
1. Well, she was just : seventeen,   and you | know what I mean,   and the
                      looked at me   and I,   I could see   that be-

| | B7 | |
way she looked was way | beyond com- | pare. | So,
fore too long I'd | fall in love with | her.

| E | E7 | A7 | C |
how could I dance | with anoth- | er, woo, | when I
She wouldn't dance | with anoth- | er, woo, | when I

| E7 | B7 | E7 | |1. |2. |
saw her | standing there. | | | 2. Well, she : | Well, my
saw her | standing there. | |

Bridge

| A7 | | |
heart went boom | when I | crossed that room,   and I

| | B7 | A7 |
held her hand | in | mine.

Verse

| E7 | | A7 |
3. Well, we danced || through the night   and we | held each other tight,

| E7 | | B7 |
and be- | fore too long I | fell in love with | her.

| E | E7 | A7 |
Now | I'll never dance | with anoth- | er, woo,

| C | E7 | B7 | E7 |
since I | saw her | standing there. | | Yeah, well since I

| B7 | A7 | E | E7 |
saw her | standing there. | | ||

6/8 TIME

A **6/8 time signature** means there are six beats in each measure, and an eighth note receives one beat. All note and rest values are proportionate to the eighth note. In other words, a quarter note receives two beats, a sixteenth note receives a half beat, and so on. Traditionally, in 6/8 time, the 1st and 4th beats are emphasized.

LUCY IN THE SKY WITH DIAMONDS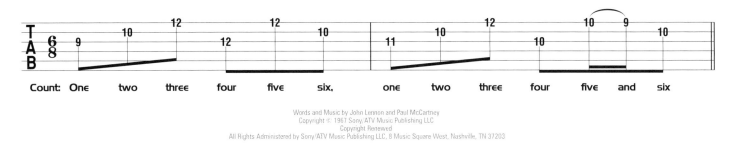

The instrumental melody in the intro of this song by the Beatles is a good example of 6/8 time. Observe the counting below the tab.

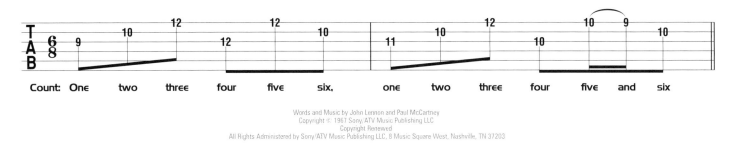

I'M SHIPPING UP TO BOSTON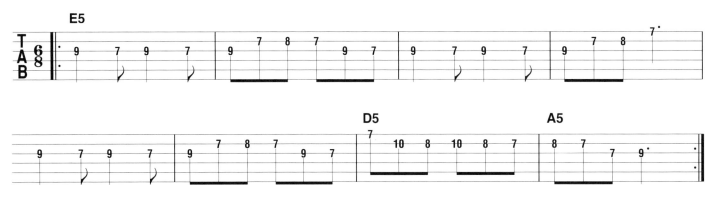

This Irish jig by the Celtic punk band Dropkick Murphys is popular at sporting events. Chord symbols are included above the staff for reference.

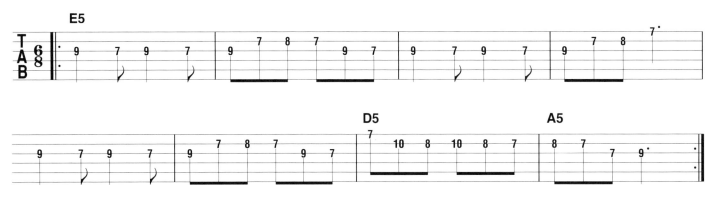

ELDERLY WOMAN BEHIND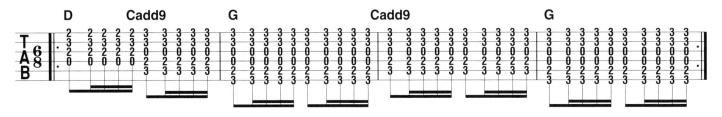
THE COUNTER IN A SMALL TOWN

Here's a Pearl Jam song in 6/8 that uses common variations of the ordinary C and G chords. The new C chord is technically called "Cadd9" because the 9th (D) is added to the basic chord. The new G chord is just an alternate voicing; instead of the open 2nd string (B), the note D is played at the 3rd fret. The new C and G chords are handy because both use the 3rd and 4th fingers to press the same notes on strings 2 and 1, respectively.

PICKING CHORDS

Strumming isn't your only option when playing chords; another way to play chords is by picking them, one note at a time. This approach offers a lighter accompaniment and works nicely for ballads.

EVERYBODY HURTS

For R.E.M.'s "Everybody Hurts," use consecutive downstrokes ( ) when picking the chords low to high, and consecutive upstrokes ( ) when picking high to low. Keep all the notes of each chord depressed so they ring together.

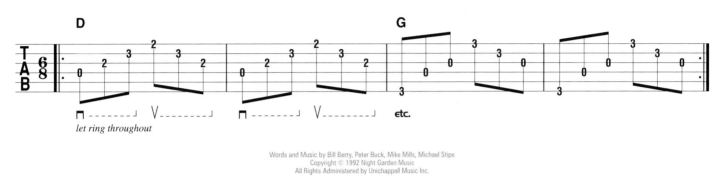

let ring throughout

HALLELUJAH

Leonard Cohen's haunting ballad has been covered many times. The picking pattern includes the note F# to connect the two chords in the main progression.

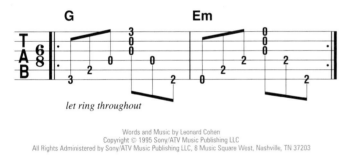

let ring throughout

BRAIN DAMAGE

Pink Floyd's song from the classic album *Dark Side of the Moon* combines chord strums and picking.

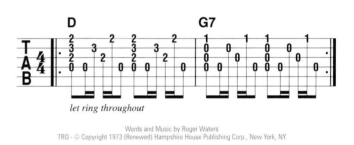

let ring throughout

THE HOUSE OF THE RISING SUN

The Animals' version of the folk classic charted in two decades, and features one of the most memorable guitar intros of all time.

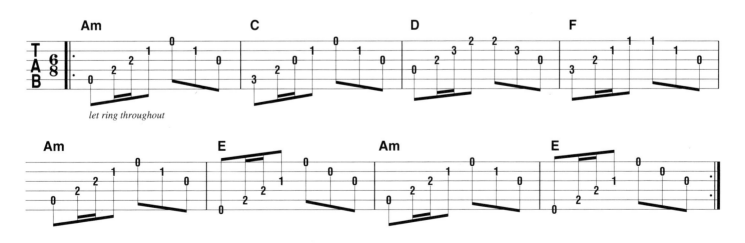

let ring throughout

THE MINOR PENTATONIC SCALE

Now that you can play chords, riffs, and rhythms, it's time to try some lead guitar. The **minor pentatonic scale** is made up of five notes, and is the scale most commonly used to create rock and blues solos. Here is the scale's movable finger pattern, which guitarists often refer to as "box position."

Minor Pentatonic Scale Pattern 1 – Root on 6th String

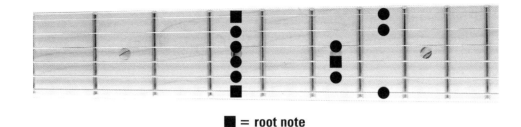

■ = root note

The pattern above can be transposed, or moved up or down the neck and played in any key. If you start the pattern with your 1st finger on the 5th fret (low A), you're playing an A minor pentatonic scale. If you move down to the 1st fret (low F), it's F minor pentatonic.

A MINOR PENTATONIC

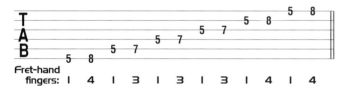

Fret-hand
fingers: 1 4 1 3 1 3 1 3 1 4 1 4

F MINOR PENTATONIC

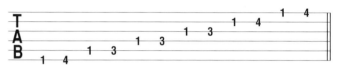

A **lick** is a short, self-contained phrase. Lead guitarists combine memorized and/or improvised licks to form a solo. Here are a few common licks derived from the minor pentatonic scale.

LICK #1
This repeating lick, based in A minor pentatonic, is a favorite of Eric Clapton.

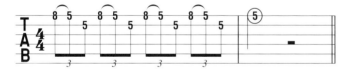

LICK #2
Here's one in the style of Led Zeppelin's Jimmy Page, also rooted in A.

LICK #3
Now let's move the "box" pattern to C (8th fret) for a lick in the style of Texas blues great Freddie King.

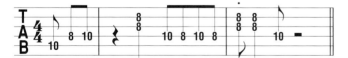

LICK #4
Rock 'n' roll legend Chuck Berry often used double stops in his solos, similar to this phrase in D.

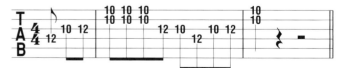

THEORY TIP

The minor pentatonic scale is built from the root, flat-3rd, 4th, 5th, and flat-7th degrees of the major scale.

C major scale =	C	D	E	F	G	A	B
	1		**♭3**	**4**	**5**		**♭7**
C minor pentatonic scale =	C		E♭	F	G		B♭

BENDING STRINGS

The **string bend** is a legato technique that produces an emotional, vocal-like sound. The fret-hand fingers push or pull the string out of its normal alignment, stretching it so the pitch of the note is raised.

Follow the steps and tab below to play your first bend. It is called a **whole-step bend** because the sound is raised to match the pitch you normally get two frets higher.

- Depress the note at the 7th fret with your 3rd finger.

- Place your 1st and 2nd fingers on the same string for support, then hook your thumb around the top of the neck for leverage.

- Pick the 3rd string and, while maintaining pressure, push "up" towards the ceiling.

Whole-Step Bend

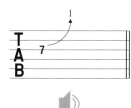

TIN PAN ALLEY
The intro to this Stevie Ray Vaughan slow blues is played in the B minor pentatonic box position.

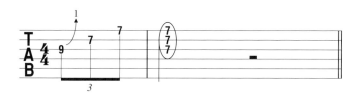

LA GRANGE
Use your 3rd or 4th finger to bend the 2nd string in this C minor pentatonic lick, which opens the solo to this ZZ Top classic.

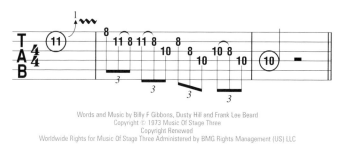

CAN'T BUY ME LOVE
Guitarist George Harrison played the solo on the Beatles' "Can't Buy Me Love" in the C minor pentatonic box position. His lead includes a **bend and release**. Pick the note, bend it, and maintain pressure as you lower the bend (without re-picking) back to its original pitch.

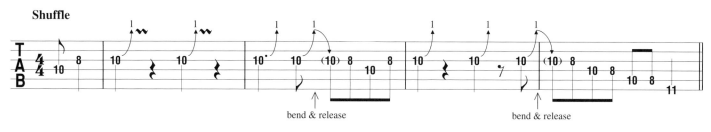

YOU GIVE LOVE A BAD NAME

The lead guitar melody in this Bon Jovi hit features a pull-off following a bend and release in the 4th measure. All of the notes are drawn from the standard C minor pentatonic box (8th fret).

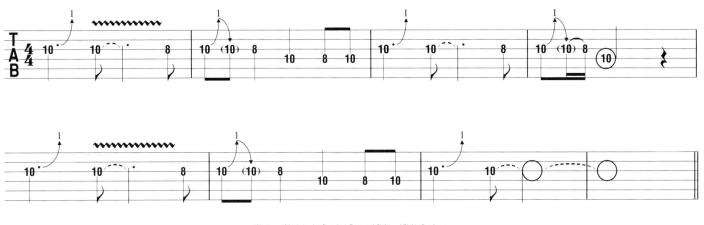

WONDERFUL TONIGHT

Eric Clapton's popular ballad features another lead melody that is great for practicing the whole-step bend and release. Listen carefully to be sure you accurately bend the note on the 10th fret (A) to match the pitch on the 12th fret (B). This example is not derived from the minor pentatonic; it uses notes from the G major scale.

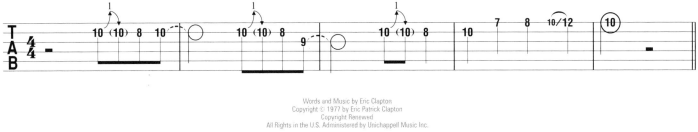

The **half-step bend** raises the pitch of a note to match the note one fret higher. The bend is played in the same manner as the whole-step bend; the string is simply not pushed quite as far.

BIRTHDAY

Here's another classic riff by the Beatles. Bend the F♯ note on the 2nd string to match the pitch of G.

BANG A GONG (GET IT ON)

Most bends are done on the first three thinner strings, but it's not uncommon to bend the low strings. For this riff by the band T. Rex, use your 2nd finger to pull the string downward, or towards the floor.

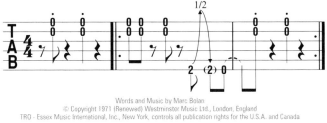

STILL GOT THE BLUES

Now let's combine whole- and half-step bends. Here is the theme to guitar great Gary Moore's poignant blues ballad.

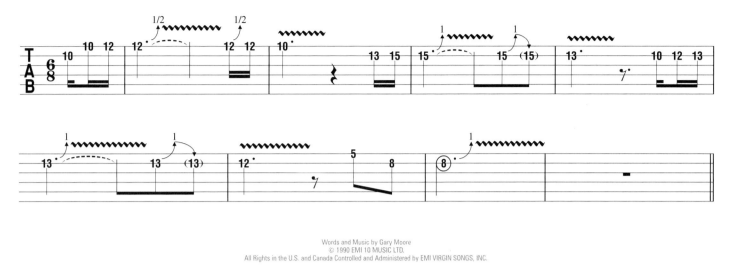

The **quarter-step bend** works well on any string and can add taste and style to a lead lick or lower-register riff. Sometimes called a "smear," this one can be played with any finger without reinforcement.

THE THRILL IS GONE

Master bluesman B.B. King plays the intro lead of his signature song using notes from the B minor pentatonic scale. He also goes beyond the basic box and extends the scale pattern with notes on the 12th fret of the 1st and 2nd strings. His mixture of quarter-, half-, and whole-step bends really makes the solo sing (and cry).

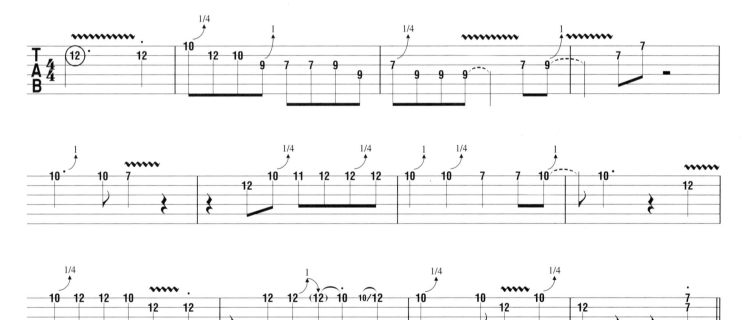

SLEEPWALK

Guitarists Jeff Beck, Larry Carlton, Joe Satriani, and Brian Setzer have recorded this instrumental hit.

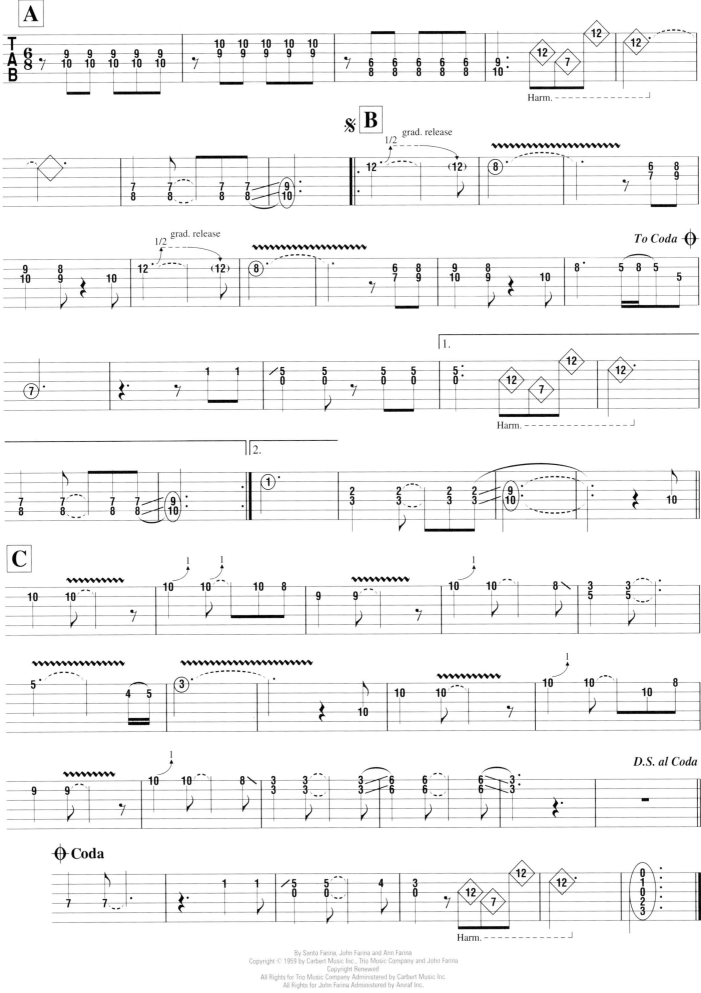